Know Your Self
for Better
Work-Life Balance

By
Sanjay Gora

Become
Shakespeare
.com

First published in 2015 by

BecomeShakespeare.com

Wordit Content Design & Editing Services Pvt Ltd.
Newbridge Business Centre, C38/39, Parinee Crescenzo Building,
G Block,Bandra Kurla Complex, Bandra East,
Mumbai 400 051, India
T: +91 8080226699

ISBN 978-93-83952-69-4

Dedicated to

My parents

Mr. Madan Lal Gora & Mrs. Kanta Devi

For giving me the gift of life

And

My wife

Mrs. Archana Gora

For giving meaning to my life.

Contents

CHAPTER 1

Photoshop Your Life

Life is a lot like photography, how you ask. Let me explain.

Move away for objectivity

I remember clicking photos from film-roll cameras way back in mid-1990s, and if we wanted a photo with some monument, we used to stand adjacent to it and take photos. I kept on doing so for many years. Then during one trip to Ajanta Ellora caves, one tourist noticed us doing that and was kind enough to point out that if we wanted a good photo of self with monument in background, we need to move away from the monument and set the frame in such a way that our close-up is taken with the monument in the background. That day and today, I still remember him with gratefulness for sharing this basic tip. I now notice others doing the same which we used to do back then but am not able to go to them and point it out. Hopefully some outgoing tourist will do that or maybe one day I will find the courage to point out.

Coming to how it applies to life, in any tricky or troubling situation, till the time we are occupied with that problem and are fire-fighting, we won't be able to overcome. We need a few moments of objective observation of the situation. For the situation to come clearly in our frame of mind, we need to move away from that for a bit and analyse it objectively. That way, things will move faster and better.

Focus better for good results

Well, we all know that. If we want to focus on a person or thing, we need to adjust our focus and concentrate on that. If we want the background to be faded, we need to take that out of focus and concentrate on the thing.

Life is a lot like that to be tackled one at a time. Whether it is, one thing at a time or one day at a time. We need to focus on our priorities in life, then only we can get better results. There is no point in trying to be jack of all (trades) and master of none.

Don't try to grab the centre

This was a tip I read in one of the articles on photography. If you want a better looking photo, try to keep the person away from the centre. Keep him on right or left, and let the background be in the other parts of the frame. This way photos will come out better and natural looking, compared to when you keep the person in the centre of the frame.

Ditto for life. If you always try to be the centre of attraction, try to grab the attention always, you will not come out natural and better looking. Just like the photos with the person in the centre, you will look as if you are posing and hogging the limelight. Try to be natural in life and let others also share the frame of life.

There is always photoshop

I used to think always that I need to go to a studio and get a good-looking photograph of me clicked with focus lights and all. This is for the cover of the book (that you are reading, so one item checked) that is on my bucket list. Then one fine day, while playing with photo editor in my phone, I used the brightness effect in a photo and lo I had the kind of picture I wanted. Easy na.

At times such is life also. You keep on thinking and planning and what not. Then suddenly one day you find there is an easier, faster and better way of doing things. Just keep going, never lose hope, persevere and one day things with be as smooth as silk.

You can photoshop your life, you know, maybe not always, but most of the times.

~ ~ ~

CHAPTER 2
The Ego Trick

"The heart has reasons that reason cannot know." -Blaise Pascal

One often comes across situations when right and left halves of the brain tell different things. That is, rational/logical half agrees with some event or person, but the emotional half (heart, if you like) does not. At such times, it is difficult to take sides, as both the halves belong to you.

And if we go by what Deepak Chopra said in the India Today Conclave recently, mind is not only your brain, but each and every cell of your body has connection with the whole, so whole body acts or reacts in every situation. That is why we say negative thoughts or contradictory thoughts create stress which release chemicals that are harmful to the body.

Then how do we overcome this duality of thought, which side we lean to. Here I would rely on Buddhist philosophy. In such situations, if we think that the problem lies with the other person, then clearly solution also lies with the other person and is beyond us.

However, if we think that problem may lie within us, then the solution is also within us and under our control.

In this context, I tried to analyse the duality of thought on the assumption that I am the one creating this duality, it is not being created by the situation *per se*. I took recourse to my home library and found a befitting explanation of what might be the root cause of this duality- Ego.

Julian Baggini explains this wonderfully in the book "The Ego Trick" as the image we may hold of ourselves may be no true reflection, but a flattering portrait produced by the magic mirror of vanity.

~ ~ ~

CHAPTER 3
Let better not be enemy of good

We were designing an advertisement for an event and there were some minor changes to be made in the final draft before putting it up for approval. Though this was just a draft and the time was very short as the boss had to leave town, arguments were taking place on using British or American English, and matching the colour scheme etc. Then I was reminded of this dialogue I heard in a TV serial last week viz. let better not be the enemy of good.

But it is easier said than done. It happens a lot. People keep sitting over the drafts for ages and when the d-day approaches, they dust the drafts and start correcting it. One can understand correcting mistakes, but making design changes, fussing over colour scheme and layout options is really irritating. If all this was to be done, this could have been done in earlier stages. Doing this in final stage only is unreasonable. But that is how it is done. Many a times, person making the changes is not doing it to harass you. It is his style, he really wants to make improvements and take it as close to perfection as possible. The problem is with his timing. But no one accepts that. Design is only one example.

This situation happens in other cases too. Over-cautious, over-perfectionist and over-meticulous people try to better their best always. There is no harm in that, till the timeline is kept in mind. However timeline is always a sideline. This delays the things instead of speeding up. Besides because of last minute changes a hundred times, the chances of mistakes creeping in increase substantially. I know from experience that this happens.

So guys, I am all with you in making improvements galore, but there comes a time when one has to say no more.

~ ~ ~

CHAPTER 4
Four Psychological Gaps

Four types of psychological gaps were mentioned in an HBR article in March,2015 issue. These psychological gaps or distance, the article explains, prevent us from attaining our goals viz. **"Gaps between yourself and other people (social distance), the present and the future (temporal distance), your physical location and faraway places (spatial distance), or imagining something and experiencing it (experiential distance)"**

I have written a lot about the social gap in my other posts, so no more dwelling on social gap here.

Coming to temporal distance, I feel that I have found a technical term for an experience I often used to have. Most of the times, while working on a designing/printing/advertising project, I had to assign deadlines for myself and my team. More often than not, the deadlines set were always wrong and got extended. Over a period of time, I started increasing the deadline estimate, added some buffer time and after several hits and trials, I could reach a stage where I was able to set deadlines realistically and targets were met. So, this overcoming of gap came with experience and over time, based on keen observation, introspection and analysis. And that I think would apply on all the four types of gaps equally.

As for spatial distance, one of my seniors taught me this by example. There was this incident when based on some news in media, we had presumed the decision to be final and issued a formal press release. Next day we came to know that the news was based on a leak, but there was some last minute change in the decision, so leak was rendered useless. That created a crisis as the issuance of press release based on leaked news was a blunder and the controlling authority was furious. My boss, who always believed in solving a crisis by physically presenting the case before the authorities took things in his hands. Before the crisis could blow over into a big one and written explanations were called for, he took me along and rushed to the office of the controlling authority. He sought time from the person in charge and put forth his explanation. He had to hear a lot, but this reduction of spatial gap averted the written explanations and actions that would have followed otherwise.

Coming to experiential distance, we wanted to introduce media buying into our company. And the way we wanted to introduce it was a first in our sector. So we were apprehensive of its actual implementation. We knew that our intentions might be questioned. So we put all our apprehensions with detailed explanations in writing as also the estimated cost savings and took approvals from the top management. We were not sure what basis could be adopted for selection of agency, as we could not decide the annual media plan in advance. We called top 10 agencies and sought their views. Ultimately the basis was finalized and approval taken. Then we were not sure, if the process would succeed at all. So we kept a provision for three-months trial period and reverting back to the old system if things did not work out. Hence foresight, research and detailed notings helped us introduce a modern, cost-effective and efficient system of media planning and buying.

The article further elaborates how one or two gaps can be compensated by reducing other gaps. And how when situation requires, gap can be increased also to meet the objectives.

~ ~ ~

CHAPTER 5

Dance of Emotions

Emotion is a tricky thing, to say the least. Each one of us has one or other set of emotions. But what makes it complex is the various levels at which emotions play with our mind- conscious, subconscious, subtle, hidden and so on. It is more like mercury-play. You press it at one point, it will pop out at another point. But when it comes to emotions, it is not as simple as that. At times, suppression, manifestation, blocking out and popping out of emotions is happening at many levels.

If you are going through a not-so-good phase in your life but are trying to somehow manage by blocking out negative thoughts or depressing vibes, you feel you have conquered your emotions. But here comes the dance of emotions in play. Without you knowing, the other emotions and feelings like anger, frustration, irritation, jumpiness start popping out often. You blame it on yourself for not being an emotionally balanced person. But in fact this is the balancing act working for you. Because you killed some emotions and tried to nip them in bud, others get stronger. As they say, if one of the five senses is weak, it is compensated by other four senses becoming better and sharper.

So when you act smart by claiming to be an emotionally strong person and not letting adversities or challenges affect you, emotions start dancing to their own tune, and you don't even get to know that you created this imbalance yourself. You may not be able to link the cause and effect, but it is there. You will snap at others, you will jump to conclusions, you will get irritated at small things. All this, because you tried to control the other emotions.

So my conclusion is, if emotions have to dance anyway, let it be free-flowing dance in their natural state than the dance resulting from imbalance or a compensatory dance, which is not in your control.

Who said, emotions are easy. The phrase "Emotional fools" can have several layers of meanings.

~ ~ ~

CHAPTER 6
Three Learnings from 3 Bosses

1991. When I started working. Have worked in two organizations since then. Three most important learnings that I got from three different bosses, thought of sharing them.

Give your juniors full scope to grow

I had joined the company just out of college and had no clue of the work environment in a company. Lucky for me I got a boss, who was a great man manager. He saw me for what I was, a small town boy, unsure of myself and not used to the ways of the big city. He taught me basics of Organization Management, the department I was posted to. But after that he never micro-managed. He used to give me an assignment and ask me to get going. At times, I was not sure and confident, then he would say in his typical Punju style

Kaka tu shuru te kar, mainu pata hai tu kar lainega (Boy, you start the job, I am sure you would do it well.)

Now I realize how he was encouraging me to learn by hit and trial. When my services were required for other departments, he used to allow me to go there. Though

I resented him for that, as I expected him to protect me from being overloading by work, specially which piled up due to laziness of other peers. But soon I found myself being sought for last-minute, rush jobs and that image still stays with me. That was his way of making me an all-rounder. When I was rotated to a different department and taken away from his tutelage, he never said a word. So he let me develop myself professionally even though it meant he would have to train another youngster to take care of his department. This quality is very rare in today›s managers. Thanks ANJ Sir.

Never lose your enthusiasm

This was the lesson given to me by a boss in my next job. He had this habit of sharing his thought process with juniors, which at that time we used to find boring. We called him a story-teller, fond of his deeds. But now I realize that he was passing on his learnings to us in an interesting manner of story telling. Or so to say verbal case studies. He was also one boss who went out of the way to help his juniors at times of personal crisis. I being an outsider in a city far-off from my hometown, this came as a blessing indeed. Another cute habit of him was that inspite of being 4-5 levels senior to us, as and when he assigned a task to us, he would say something like- Sanjay, would you do this please? As if I had a choice. But this made us felt so valued and respected that we gave our best always. Before coming to his life lesson to me, one more thing. He always used to say if someone invites you to his family function, please don't take it lightly. Feel blessed that out of 300-400 people he thought of sharing his happiness with, one is you. So make it a point to be there. And a point he did make when he went to one of the weddings, almost straight out of a hospital. Leading by example, you say.

One fine day when I was a bit upset and was sitting with him in his chamber. He read my mood and told me, Sanjay, if there is one lesson I am asked to give to anybody at work, I would say-Never lose your enthusiasm. If your enthusiasm is gone, everything is gone. There is no point of you working anymore. And what a lesson indeed. He shared many examples from his life when any other man might have given up, but he never let it affect his enthusiasm. We saw him practicing the maxim day in and day out. And maybe that is why the lesson has stayed with me. Thanks JCM Sir.

No compromise on your principles

This boss played a big role in my life. I was living away from parents and he was instrumental in bringing me back to a place near my hometown. He took a liking to me and helped me in many ways on personal and work front. So he is one of the few persons in my life, I will ever be grateful to. He mentored me in the domain of communication at corporate level, as opposed to my experience at unit level. He did this by giving me a free-hand, taking me in his secretariat and empowering me. This way I could get exposure to most of the functions in a corp-comm setup in a short period of time. One feels blessed at times how some seniors take you under their wings and make you learn and grow to your potential. I wasnotawarethatIwasgoingthroughthistransformation until very late in my career. There were many who felt envious and badmouthed me. But he never bothered. I continued to work hard and never indulged in these shenanigans and maybe that won him over. He is the one who taught me to always be a thorough professional and never ever compromise on your principles. You are my role model in professionalism. Thanks DR Sir.

Learning is still on. But I would rather wait and share learnings from present bosses after some years. Else I would be branded as you know what.

~ ~ ~

CHAPTER 7
Ten positive emotions

I was watching videos of a courser (MOOC) course on positive psychology and the course faculty explained how negativity bias results in immediate outcome. Whereas positive emotions are momentary with outcomes setting in after a long time.

She described 10 positive emotions, most of which we might not even notice as positive emotions. These are

Joy	Pride
Gratitude	Amusement
Serenity	Inspiration
Interest	Awe
Hope	Love.

You can google the course if interested.

What interested me in this list was that in reality I never thought of most of these emotions as having a positive effect. At best, neutral. I took amusement to be the most visible sign of happiness and often blamed myself for not being happy enough.

But going by the list of positive emotions, I found myself awash with many of the emotions. Of course, without realising that these had a positive psychological effect.

Gratitude is one. I always pride myself for being sincere in my gratitude. I still remember with fondness the kind acts by friends 20 years back. I may not have reciprocated the same but in my heart of heart, I am ever grateful to people who unselfishly helped me at times of need. I used to think that I overdo it sometimes. But now I know better.

Serenity is a manifestation of introversion which I excel at, so tick that too.

Interest. Give me a book or an interesting TV series and you have me hooked.

Hope is my hallmark to the extent of hopelessness.

Inspiring me is difficult as I have very high standards of expectations. But I do have role models, so check that too.

My kind of love is pure, unadulterated and unconditional care.

So 6/10 is not bad.

I am sure most of you would also be experiencing these emotions on a daily basis. Just note the positive nature of these emotions and you will realize how unaware we are about ourselves.

CHAPTER 8
Borrowed Happiness

"The natural flights of the human mind are not from pleasure to pleasure, but from hope to hope." - Samuel Johnson

Recently I was expecting news of a big accomplishment. All the i's were dotted and t's were crossed. Things were going on smoothly. The task was happening in stages, and with successful completion of every stage the chances of success were improving. So as the task progressed, I started building hopes of successful completion. This resulted in an expectation-soaked feeling of happiness. With each stage, the barometer of happiness kept moving up. So much so that, I started planning a treat for the team after the task was done. When we entered the penultimate stage in the task, I could feel tinge of ecstasy knocking on the door. Two weeks were left for the deadline. Our adviser was cautioning us to stay balanced. But we went ahead with our planning for celebrations and jubilation. The goal was so near that it blurred our vision. We were so engrossed in our over-confidence and positivity that we put caution aside. I did not want any pessimism to overshadow my happy mood. I enjoyed complete bliss in those last few days with my hope and expectation of successful accomplishment. But in the end, the task was a failure and we did not succeed.

However the happiness that we experienced while waiting for the result is beyond words. I am not sure we would have experienced more happiness, had we succeeded.

So this borrowed-happiness for 15 days will stay with us for ever. I am saying this for a reason. A similar incident happened with me in 2003.

I was trying for transfer from Rourkela to Delhi. I was told that it has happened and my transfer order should be on its way. In the evening, I and wife discussed plans for moving to Delhi. We relived the 6 years we had spent in Rourkela and kept on deliberating related things for 2 hours. I still remember vividly the rooftop, the cool breeze, the shared laughter, the nostalgic memories, the micro-planning, the whole episode. Next day I got to know that my transfer has been cancelled after some internal politics by some people.

In this case also, the result was not good, but those two hours are precious memories for me till date. As will these 15 days be. Call me whatever, but this borrowed happiness stays. I don't know the logic and rationale for this, but I do know for sure that it does. I did get that transfer three years later though.

~ ~ ~

CHAPTER 9
Transference Trap at Work

Transference is the term for continuity between early childhood and adult behaviour as we all bring to our current relationships a map of past relationships that we transfer onto the present. This was explained by Manfred FR Kets de Vries in an article and he further explained-This particularly happens during times of stress and in hierarchical situations. Indeed, people in positions of authority have an uncanny ability to reawaken transferential processes in themselves and others. And these reactions can present themselves in a number of ways-positively or negatively. The confusion of time and place results in psychic noise at the workplace. Freud, who formulated this concept, was not interested in business. But it would have been fascinating to see what sense he would have made of everyone's tendency in business to relate to people as if they were someone else.

From my personal experience, transference at work has been negative for me. I related to some peers as siblings I never had but ended up burning my fingers. But I myself was at fault in doing so, as I blurred the personal and professional distinction. I used to impose my imaginary relation onto them overtly or covertly. Then in my utopian dreams, I expected them to reciprocate those feelings, which was very foolish of me. Secondly, it started to cloud my professional assessment and interactions with them. I found myself being overly sentimental about small things and started expecting a lot from them, which was unreasonable. When they behaved normally and treated me like any other colleague would, I felt cheated. Being an introvert, I retracted back to my shell but that did not help. In all such cases, the catharsis happened when I jerked myself out of the transference trap. That put an end to my exaggerated expectations from them and brought me back to the real world.

Learning never stops really. Waiting to learn from and share other of my follies in the realm of homo sapiens.

~ ~ ~

CHAPTER 10
To bypass hierarchy or not

This question has been troubling me for last couple of years, as I see different bosses adopting opposite strategies. Few bosses go strictly by the rules. They assign job to their immediate juniors and then take feedback from them. The other indirect team members are assigned tasks by their immediate seniors. Top boss never assigns the job directly to them. This is clear to understand theoretically at least.

The other strategy is of heads who feel, rightly or wrongly, that it is their responsibility to mentor each and everyone. This is specially applicable to departments where there are 20-30 officers in different ranks and reporting structures. So the HOD assigns tasks right, left and center, to direct, indirect, lateral reports. This creates confusion and chaos. But the positive side is that boss is directly getting to interact with youngsters and is able to assess their strengths and capabilities. Youngsters get to have a say to the person who matters. In an organization, where HOD gets to have a say in final appraisal grades, irrespective of assessment by reporting officers, this matters more. In this system, middle bosses can't succeed in creating image of juniors the way they want. They can't grab credit for all jobs done by their juniors. The juniors get to be mentored by a senior official with more age and more experience and more say in their career development. This also flattens the hierarchy and their is no middle fat in functioning. One job is likely to be done by one person and not 3-4 persons working together or pretending to work together. All this is the good side.

The flip side of direct delegation is also there. Once or twice it is okay. But by doing so frequently, HOD is undermining the authority of reporting officers. I have seen HOD assigning the jobs to junior without keeping his boss in loop. And then asking the boss about update on the job. When this happens, juniors also start taking the boss for granted and prefer doing only those things that HOD directly assigns them. HOD ends up taking responsibility for all the jobs that he is directly assigning. HOD is also creating precedents which can create problems later.

Now, if there are 3-4 direct reports to HOD and one of them is not a good supervisor, HOD can take the command of that team in his hands directly. But he would be doing that at the cost of not professionally developing that supervisor. But if an HOD does it as a habit with all his direct reports, I think he is at fault.

I faced this peculiar situation in my previous stint at my job. Not only was it irritating, demotivating and unsettling, it also led to decrease in overall efficiency of the team, in my view at least.

~ ~ ~

CHAPTER 11
One at a time

One at a time. Well, it can be one day or one thing, but at a time.

Following the dictum of one day at a time is basically convincing your mind to not wander to past troubles or future worries. Rather live in the present, or so to say, one day at a time. More about that some other day.

Here I want to write about doing one thing at a time. And ironically this goes against the gist of another chapter which highlights the virtues of multitasking. Actually I read somewhere how doing one thing at a time is more effective. As it means you are giving full attention and focus to that one thing at a given moment. So your whole mental energy is directed to that one thing. You are not giving 1/10th of attention to 10 different things at one time. You are not letting outside things like phone, visitors, messages disturb you. Then once that one thing has been taken care of, you move on to the next thing and give it full attention. This saves your energy and time as you don't have to do things again and again or restart from the beginning due to lack of focus. That leads to duplication, overlap and confusion. I found the argument very convincing. Especially because at my workplace, I get to meet such a person who is an embodiment of this dictum. The level of attention he gives to each and every person or issue, is remarkable. Initially I got the wrong impression that I am one of the lucky recipients of his focus. But later I realized that undivided attention to issue at hand is his hallmark of excellence. I am now trying to work on myself to develop this habit. This in other words implies giving respect to time of other person.

But I do rethink at times if I shift my loyalty to concepts and move from one to other too fast. What is your take on choosing between multitasking and one-thing-at-a-time?

~ ~ ~

CHAPTER 12
Self-motivation
a la Indian Poets

Have you ever attended a poets' meet in India? If yes, you would know what I am talking about. If no, you must attend one to learn the art of soliciting forced compliments.

A typical poet would start his recitation by asking the audience to encourage him by clapping together. Then before every small couplet, he will say- I would like your attention (read claps) to the next couplet. This can have many variations like

- You are a very attentive / intelligent / wise / literate / cooperative audience, so I am sure you would appreciate me

- Those who are able to understand the intensity of my writing would applaud, others would not (meaning that they are not smart enough)

- This city has always been responsive to my creations, so today I expect the same.

- I would like your appreciation for my meaningful poetry

- If I am able to get across my deep social message to you, I would expect applause

- If my satire or pun touches your funny bone, do let me know by clapping

- I would like you all to sing along with me

- Please say attaboy (wahwah) after my each sentence

The list goes on.

What I want to pinpoint here is, what if we could emulate this strategy at work. Easier said than done, I know.

But imagine, before starting every small task, you ask your boss to notice how adept and proficient you are. You ask him to pat your back or compliment you profusely if you do well. You ask your juniors to observe your actions carefully, as there will be gems of wisdom flowing from your sneezes and yawns. Your writing is no less than Shakespeare and words flowing from your mouth are scriptures.

If your colleagues don't appreciate you loudly, you make fun of them and laugh at their stupidity.

If we compare a poet and an officer, it will be like

Now I am opening my PC, applause

Now Making a new excel file, applause

Now entering data and making tables, applause

Now I am blah, blah, blah... Get my point.

Any volunteers for the strategy?

~ ~ ~

CHAPTER 13
Is Trust over-rated?

We had been going to a hospital for medical treatment for few consecutive days. The treating physician was a gem of a person. In fact, she was the reason for our starting treatment from that hospital. But when her staff asked us to take medicines from hospital dispensary only, I was a bit taken aback. True, she never asked us to do it, but staff had her tacit assent. Now knowing her, we concluded that she must be ensuring that the treatment does not get affected by the spurious drugs bought from outside. However, there was this lurking doubt at the back of our mind, that hospital, if not the doctor, was interested in revenues from the medicines sold.

In another instance, while undergoing this treatment, we had to get some tests done from some lab. We went to India's most reputed pathlab. Since there were many tests, I went to a collection centre and asked for estimate and other details. The guy gave me the same. Later on when I actually went for the tests in the Main lab, the receptionist sounded very cooperative and genuine, and asked me to take customised test-packages as it would be cost-effective. I consented and was all praise for her.

Later when I totalled the bills, I found out that she had taken more than the estimate.

Perchance both the cases with trust issues pertained to Medical field. But it happens in almost every domain.

In life, one starts trusting individuals and systems but then when that trust is broken, one feels like doubting oneself and one's judgement. You then decide that you won't trust anybody from now on. But then if you are an incorrigible optimist like me, you fall into the trust trap again and again.

Is trust over-rated? We should rather have no trust on anybody? But then, is such a world even possible, where no one trusts no one.

~ ~ ~

CHAPTER 14
Play the Game

A recent issue of HBR magazine had a wonderful article-The Authenticity Paradox.

The idea in brief as explained in the magazine is-When we view authenticity as an unwavering sense of self, we struggle to take on new challenges and bigger roles. The reality is that people learn-and change-who they are through experience.

The solution HBR suggests is- by trying out different leadership styles and behaviors, we grow more than we would through introspection alone. Experimenting with our identities allows us to find the right approach for ourselves and our organizations.

Call it serendipity or what, I was analysing and introspecting on my thought process in dealing with a senior colleague last week. Unexpected lies, indifference, overly self-centric actions and absence of a sense of responsibility were irritating me. But I knew I was being too fussy and over-reactive. Now, since problem was mine, I had to find a permanent solution to this. I worked on different phrases that I could use for myself in situations involving the colleague which irritated me, e.g. stop being a fool, don't expect anything, everyone has moods, tit for tat, expect nothing less, more to come, don't bother and a new relation with self. But nothing seemed to hit the nail on the head. Then cropped up the three words in my mind

Play the Game

This sounded great and is working for awkward situations. And then I got to read this article, which basically suggests the same.

In my effort to be authentic to myself, I was being too rigid, as rightly pointed out in this article. I wanted to be straightforward, tell-all kind of person and expected others to be same. But real world is not custom made for me. I need to customize myself to others, to adapt. There is no point in sulking and cribbing. Rather, take the absurdities and shenanigans as a challenge and play the game.

Being authentic does not mean being fixated with self notions. This is what I learnt from the article and I am a slow learner, you see. It is rare that one single article can change your thinking in such a way. Till I read this article, I did consider introspection as the best way to improve yourself. But as the article points out, which self you are introspecting on. It keeps changing. So play the game. Thanks to the author Herminia Ibarra.

~ ~ ~

CHAPTER 15

Value your values

Life is easy if you know what your life values are. These can be money, prestige, peace, family, love, care, the list is endless. But you need to prioritise. You may say that I want them all, but then these will not be your life values, but your needs.

And as they say in management assessment tests or behavioural analysis, no answer is right or wrong. Your answer, if given truly can reveal much about yourself. You need not tell anybody if you don't want to. But You will know a lot of what defines your personality and your actions.

For example, if mental peace and easy going life is your life value, that will explain your lack of ambition, absence of killer instinct and your balanced personality.

If money is your primary concern in life, you will have a dream of your own business some time in life, if you don't have it now. It will explain your risk-taking, your burning midnight oil and your hunger for more.

If following creative pursuits or getting recognition in society is your life value, then your actions and reactions will speak for themselves.

What this does is that it makes things easier for you. In difficult situations, you can use the life value as yardstick and choose the right course of action. It enables you to be at ease with yourself. And that my friends, is a big thing.

Other thing that valuing your values can do for you is to understand your actions in retrospect. That again is of great help in understanding and improving your working style, if you want to.

Do you?

~ ~ ~

CHAPTER 16
Choose to be happy

I said it. Finally. We tend to blame others for our problems, our life issues. It is either our parents, friends, bosses, juniors or others who are the real reason for our troubles. Never us. We are perfect. Are we?

That is what I am trying to explore here. No, we are not perfect and no one is, for that matter. But that does not stop us from blaming others for our predicament. My boss makes me stay beyond office hours. I don't get the preferential treatment that others get. Why does he listen to him, but not me. They must be well-connected going by the perks they get. She is growing fast in her career because she is a woman and I am not.

All these shitty thoughts are what keeps us away from happiness. Come to think of it and you would realize that none of this is true. As they say it's choices and chances that make your life. That applies to big things in life and small too. For example, if you are staying beyond office hours, it is ultimately your choice. You may have your reasons for doing so, but the choice is yours. If you feel you have been sidelined or ignored, have you really spoken it out loud, or sulking has been your way out. I can bet it's the latter. Else you would have got your way. My boss once said about me to someone, "He can not raise his voice. I have done injustice to him several times, but he has never uttered a word about that." I am never proud of this statement. It speaks more about the choices I make than my cool temper.

At times, I find people comparing what others are doing in office. So you hear statements like, he gossips and roams around all day, while I slog for hours together. That again is a very negative choice you make. Of letting you be swayed by the choices others make. My simple counter to such thoughts is to tell yourself that you are being paid to work for the hours that you put in. You are working for yourself, for the salary. You need not compare yourself with others. Yes, if you end up working overtime because of this situation then you need to escalate the issue. But if you are able to manage to work from 9 to 5, and need not stretch yourself, then there is no point in making comparisons. Just be true to yourself.

At times you see people less talented than you moving up fast. You and everyone else knows that the sole reason is their ability to suck up and the willingness of sucked-ones to favour the suckers. That is that. Now make it clear to yourself that not sucking up is your choice. There is no point in being envious. You had been in that guy's place, had you chosen to suck up. But you did not, so that is a healthy choice you made, now stick to it, own it up and be strong about it.

You did not compromise on your life values, and that is your takeaway. Let it be that way.

CHAPTER 17

Give time some time

I have seen from experience that sometimes, the big stress was just a bubble created by a misunderstanding. So best way to avoid such situations is to chill for some time. Many a times, we jump to conclusions too soon. We weave stories in our minds about what could have and would have happened.

If XYZ are laughing loudly and looking at you, they must be laughing at you. If A fought with you and went to B, he must be bitching about you to B. If I don't get this assignment, my job will be at stake. If boss is calling A and not calling B, Boss must be angry with B.

Boss did not talk to me and did not respond to my smile, I must have done something terrible. XYZ are missing together, they must be doing some scheming against me. You can keep on adding to this list of instances where our mind wanders unhindered and creates a pool of negative thoughts from which we cannot seem to come out. In such situations, my advice would be to give time some time. At times, circumstances make you realize that you were shooting in the dark. On some occasions, the persons you were thinking of, themselves clear your doubts and apprehensions.

And rest of the times, if you give time some time, you realize after a few days that you were fretting over nothing. On several occasions, things take care of themselves. You just need to deliberately take your mind off the troubling thoughts. Let the things be. In due course of time, the pieces fall into place and you get the bigger picture.

Long back in my previous posting, I was set in my ways and was enjoying the daily routine I had adjusted to. One fine day, boss calls and tells me-CEO has decided to post you to another unit. It came as a shock. I expected boss to have defended me and fought for me. Since nothing of that sort happened, I joined the new unit and stayed there for 2 years. I learnt new technical skills in that unit, which are useful in my present assignments. So a job I hated and disliked as I felt dumped there, proved to be a new training ground. After several years, CEO told me that I was specially picked up and posted in the unit to bring in improvements. Now at that time, neither CEO nor boss told me that. There was no doubt a communication gap. But in retrospect, I realize that giving time some time is helpful. I now thank my stars, for having been posted in the unit. Times does take care of everything. Time out, for now.

CHAPTER 18
Fighting stress physically

Well, almost physically. People do different things when they are stressed out. Here is what I could gather from different sources about what all we can do physically, as opposed to mentally, to overcome stress.

Sleep it off- My favourite. More because sleep is my favourite pastime, stress or no stress. I can say with confidence that if you can manage this, nothing like that. Now there may be people with insomnia or so much stress that they can't even think of sleeping. For them, this may not work. But for others, this is wonderful. Have a good night's sleep or a day's as the case maybe, and you are sure to wake up in a better frame of mind.

Walk over it- Not literally of course. But walking does relieve your body and mind, specially when you are stressed. So does exercise. Gym and myself have no relation at all, so I can not say with personal experience. But friends have told me that exercise is very effective in stress control. There is some chemical relation between physical exercise and stress relief. But let us leave that to medical professionals. Test for yourself. Punching bags are also an exercise. Voodoo dolls, hmm, not sure.

Talk it over- Yes, at times, best remedy is to take the bull by the horns. When a person or situation is causing you regular stress, go to the person who can make a difference. Compose yourself, gather your thoughts, rein in your emotions, practice what you will say and get going. There can be two possibilities. Either the person will help you, which is very good. But even if he does not, you will at least have the satisfaction of calling a spade a spade. You can also say all those things, which our mind keeps telling itself- I could have said this, I should have said this.

Do good- Compassion is considered to be a recharger for a stressed mind. Doing good to others makes you happy with yourself. Don't believe me, try doing it yourself. It has to be an unselfish act though, for the effect to be complete. And if you have made a habit of helping others, you will do it even when you are stressed. The positive chemicals, ya I know, yet again, will balance out the negative thingy. Some sympathetic and parasympathetic nervous system drama. But who cares. Results speak for themselves.

~ ~ ~

CHAPTER 19
Tips for instant stress management

I know, I know, it sounds childish to claim instant stress management *a la* 2-minute instant noodles or instant coffee. But what I am talking about is short-term control, enabled by your own internal stress fighting mechanism. For long term stress management, one needs a long term strategy.

In spite of all your efforts, you can not not have stress at all. Rather it is good to have stress at times, good stress, as it helps you respond and perform better in some situations. But when you feel that stress is not letting you think and work properly, here are some tips and tricks, used by me and my friends (who shared these with me) for instant stress management.

Take deep breaths for 2-3 minutes. It will calm your mind 100 per cent, if only for few minutes. This has something to do with more oxygen going in and all that. I won't stress your already stressed mind with scientific data, you can always google it, if you want to know more.

Vent it out. Have a trusted colleague/friend in or nearby your office. Dump all your worries on him. What happens at times is that while retelling the episode that is bothering you, you yourself realize that you are over-reacting. That cools you down. At other times, narrating the incident/problem, lets you push your anger out and soothes your nerves.

Smile it away. I have recently started using this trick. You must have heard the saying that it is easy to tolerate many things but tolerating bullshit is not that easy. And there are many intellectuals roaming around eager to shower their knowledge on other poor earthlings. You will find equal number of over-smart people ready with their wisecracks and silly interventions. Earlier I used to snap at them and cut them short. This mostly resulted in spoiling the working relationships which caused problems later on. Now whenever I come across such jerks, I don't react instantly. I force myself to bring a smile, which naturally tones down my retort, if any. I heard someone saying once- you only have to paste a smile on your face and keep your volume down, then you can say virtually anything to anybody.

Listen to music. Music has many powers. Stress management is one. But you will have to prepare in advance. Think over the songs that relax you. Spiritual, ghazals, soft songs, fast, instrumental, classical, whatever helps you. Then make a folder of such songs that you like. The objective of this folder is to use it when you want instant relief. Because you have researched already based on your preferences, this will come in handy when you really need it.

Read fiction that you like. This may not be possible in all situations. But if and when you can, use it. And if you have been reading a novel, thriller and can start off from where you left, it will be more engrossing and take your mind off the stress. If you like reading, of course.

So, what is your poison?

~ ~ ~

CHAPTER 20
Glass Half-full of Milk

We have heard the oft-quoted example of positive thinking viz. a glass filled to half level. An optimist will see it as a glass half-full and a pessimist will see it as a glass half-empty. But life is never as simple as that. There are several shades of gray between black and white. So here let me share two variations. One is that even the so-called empty half is not really empty; it is filled with life-sustaining air. And the second is of a glass half-filled with milk. To a person who likes milk, the filled portion will be an incentive. And to a person who does not like milk, the empty portion will be an incentive. Who said life was simple.

Well, the point I am trying to make here is you need to have a positive frame of mind. And the definition of such a mind state will vary from person to person. You have to devise your own modus operandi. The best way to always stay positive is to look for positives even in negative situations. That may sound selfish and mean, but it is not. What it implies basically is that you observe a disturbing situation from an objective state of mind and search for possible positive outcomes deliberately.

You may feel like you are adopting an escapist route, but if stress management is your goal, then this is the best alternative in any given work situation. Once when I started working with a new boss, he changed the job profiles of all persons in the department. I was handling coveted assignments prior to this. All these jobs were taken away from me and I was given entirely new set of assignments. Now I could sulk and sulk for ever or adapt to the new scenario. After the initial shock, I introspected and realized that new assignments would help learn new things, make me better-equipped for higher jobs and give some free time for personal life. Once I reached these conclusions, life was easier for me then on. The new boss had another habit of sharing info with team on need-to-know basis. Earlier boss shared most of the things with me so I was privy to important info always. This new scenario initially bothered me. But gradually I came to realize that in earlier regime, with every piece of info, came the responsibility of being a part of each and every ongoing assignment. I could never say no, even when my personal life was affected a lot. The new boss ensured that each person gets equitable workload. Once I narrowed down the situation to this positive outlook, I lived happily ever after, okay, till the new boss stayed. While I was writing this, I got a message on whatsapp-Everything in the world is beautiful depending on the context. A school bell sounds irritating at 8 am but the same sounds melodious at 2 pm. So, do you like milk?

~ ~ ~

CHAPTER 21

Choose your God

As if. Well, when I say choose your god or godman for that matter, what I mean is, more as a matter of somebody to rely on rather than being religious.

You see, more than 90 per cent of the people believe in one god or another. It may be Jesus, Krishna, Allah and so on. There are living godmen in India who head different sects and teach ways to meet God. You may agree or disagree with their principles and teachings. But one thing is common among them. They teach you to have faith, trust, belief in one superpower, the supreme creator, known by different names in different religions. They want you to have complete faith in his doing and have patience. Whatever happens, it happens for your own good. The god gives you what you need, not what you want. You live happily and peacefully in whatever condition he puts you in. If there are adversities, these make you stronger. Then there is the concept of Karma and reincarnation. As you sow, so shall you reap. The list of preaching's is endless.

My point here is that all god-fearing people and believers tend to believe in all such teachings. God's fear is a good torch-bearer for them in their life's journey. So if you are a believer already, try to strengthen your beliefs and at times of stress, rely on these time-tested philosophies. Mind works in strange ways. But what has been drilled into the psyche for generations and is reinforced through sermons and teachings will be a great soothing force at times of chaos. You leave all the worries to this superpower and keep doing your work. And if you have been brought up in a religious environment, practicing this won't be a problem for you. Your mind is readymade and custom-trained for such reliance on god. Just use it at the right time in a right way in right doses. If a living guru or spiritual guide inspires such trust and respect in you, no worries. Let him be bearer of your burdens at times of crisis. That will lessen your stress and tension to a great extent.

Coming from an agnostic like me, believing in a superpower, even if for selfish reasons of stress management should be easy, no. And let us assume there is no super power, even then what is the harm if it helps relieve your worries.

~ ~ ~

CHAPTER 22
Give stress some stress

Counterintuitive you say. Not really. What it means is having an allotted time for stressful thoughts. There may be several days when some persons or some actions are causing you a lot of stress. On those days, the normal reaction is to shut out such stressful thoughts. At times, we succeed, but mostly we don't. Negative, stressful thoughts are like vicious loops and traps, which don't let us come out of the cyclone of repetitive, frustrating and crappy feelings. So don't try and suppress them, let them come to the surface, float harmlessly in your mind space, while you try switching to a different mode.

And what can help doing that is setting a fixed time slot for stress management. Once your mind knows that you are not going to ignore things that are bothering it, rather you are allotting full 30 minutes exclusively for it, the mind will allow you to do other jobs peacefully. But take care to allot a time when you are really likely to be free and think about the stressful persons and situations in a comprehensive manner. Don't try to go back on your promise, don't fool and don't cheat your mind. It will know, it's your mind after all.

So during the slotted hour, take out all your worries and allow them to bombard you with all the questions. Let what-if be given full freedom to dance. Let only-if be the show stealer. Apply all suggested tricks of the trade elsewhere. Whether it is one problem that is troubling you, or a couple of them, let your mind be the class monitor. But keep yourself focussed enough to come up with a rationale for what is troubling you and how best you can manage your mind to prevent it from becoming a constant irritation and nuisance. Adopt flow chart, tree diagram and other such techniques to have a response to all possible scenarios.

Believe me once you have done that, it will be stress that will run for a hiding place, not you.

~ ~ ~

CHAPTER 23
When stressed, think of worse

What the heck is he talking about? Well call it contrarian or whatever, but thinking of worse-that-can-happen at times of stress is a sure shot cure for minimising stress. Yep, I am talking of worst case scenario. In most of the stress-causing scenarios, extreme outcome would be much less than death, the ultimate fear of homo sapiens. And once that realization dawns, stress flies away.

Don't believe me? Try for yourself. Boss has shouted at you, junior has in-subordinated, assignment getting delayed, committed a mistake, got fooled, not promoted, transferred to a new section/location. It can go on and you can add your stressors here. Point is to make yourself think of worst that could happen, when any of these situations is troubling you. You will always reach the conclusion that this is not the worst that could happen to me. Now no one is saying you surrender to circumstances and be a hopeless realist. No, the imagining of worst case scenario is to help you emerge out of stress loop that you have entangled yourself in.

Once you have introspected in such a way, analysed the situation from all possible angles, pondered over all possible outcomes and finally arrived at the conclusion that things could be worse, you will be a different person. First, by comparing the feared outcome to worst outcome, you allay your apprehensions. Second, when you think of realistically possible outcome, you become fearless and you can move on to better things at work. You can concentrate on your work. Even if at later stages, fears and stress try to crop up again in your mind, you can always brush them away with worst-case-ruled-out scenario.

Our mind does play weird games. But once we tame this beast, it is fun.

~ ~ ~

CHAPTER 24
What is eating you?

What is eating you?

This must be the first lesson of stress management-101. If we can objectively analyse our reaction to a person or an incident and narrow down the rationale of our stress, logical or illogical, half the problem is solved. Rest half is the left-out strategies of stress management.

But easier said than done, because it is not as simple as it sounds. To-each-his-own factor complicates the situation. Given similar situations, one person may stress himself to hospital, and another can just laugh it off. So there is no one solution that fits all. It will depend on your upbringing, your nature-introvert or extrovert, your level of maturity, your belief in Karma and a super power (God maybe), your family values, your life goals, your temperament- the list goes on.

Moreover, to pinpoint the cause of your stress requires, accepting your weaknesses and shortcomings. Not everyone can do that. We see ourselves with coloured glasses. We can justify our prejudices, our biases, our mistakes wonderfully.

So what can cause stress? Lot of things, like jealousy, ego, greed, ambition, competition, to name just a few.

A friend of mine claims and pretends to be almost a reincarnation of Buddhha, the supreme controller of emotions, feelings and senses. But when it comes to stress at work, he is no better than you or me. He got all his promotions in time, has the confidence of his seniors and respect of his juniors, but still insecurities eat his brain away. He knows he has no competition from his team as he is in higher grade, still he is anxious. He knows likings and appreciation from seniors are momentary and transitory, still he covets them.

So it is very difficult for him to assess most of the times what is eating him away. It can not be jealousy, because there is nothing to envy. It is not backstabbing and backbiting, since he himself promotes and highlights his team. It can not be ego, since he has risen above all this (or has he?) He keeps on cancelling out all probable causes and is left with a stress without a reason. Told you it was not easy. So he repeats the process and after several rounds of introspection, arrives at the cause of his stress. At times, it is fear of change, fear of unknown and at times it is fear of known and dreaded. At times, it is latent craving for recognition, at others it is suppressed desire for popularity and visibility. He also aspires to be always in the good books of people who matter, but does not want to suck up.

Who said life at work is a joy ride. But let me assure you, when he is able to narrow down to his poison, he is relieved of half the stress. For the other half, well that is a long story.

~ ~ ~

CHAPTER 25
Handshakes and Shakehand

"Who does not dislike a boneless hand extended as though it were a spray of sea-weed, or a miniature boiled pudding? It is equally annoying to have one's hand clutched aloft in grotesque affectation." While reading this quote by Emily Post, variety of handshakes come to mind. I am sure you must have experienced some if not all the types.

SLIMY FINGERS

Some people have this tendency of offering forefinger or two fingers half-heartedly as if shaking hand would reduce their life span by half. What hole their fingers are trying to find, it is difficult to understand. If you have to show middle finger and mean up-yours, have the guts to say it. If you want to poke or scratch, find the right place. But have the decency to shake hands properly, else don't do it.

ITCHY SHAKE

You will be shocked when you experience this shake for the first time, if you have not already. The guy offers his hand nicely, but when your palms meet, he suddenly curls his forefinger and starts scratching your palm. You will think it's by mistake or he is just having fun. But I am told this means the guy wants you to engage in underhand dealings and is offering quid pro quo. Strange are the ways of the corrupt.

JET SHAKE

This guy is in a lot of hurry. Will say hi, offer hand and then move on to next person. But he does it in such a hurry that you feel like grabbing him by neck and ask him to shake hands properly. What happens is he will say hi and offer his hand and by the time you raise your head and try to meet his eyes, he has moved on to the next person. At times, his hand still stays offered for you to take and complete the greeting, while he has started talking to the next person. I for one don't leave his hand till such time that he is confused and looks at me with a question-mark and I get to tell him to shake hand properly or not do at all. After that, they at least try to pretend or make fun of my reminder, by feigning over-courteousness, but remember they do.

FOREARM SHAKE

You will find this very common in India. The guy is coming out of wash room or after having meals. He will not say his hands are wet, dirty or oily. He will just extend his forearm to you, even if you seem least inclined to shake hands and show no interest by offering one. And you are supposed to grab his forearm and complete the greeting. He behaves as if you are impatient to shake hands with him, or he is so busy that he can greet you just now and not after. Please somebody tell such people that it is called handshake for a reason.

WRESTLER SHAKE

Somebody please tell them firm does not mean 500 kg/square metre pressure. Firm means full grip and confident grasp. They think it is a match of physical strength and the one who presses the hardest is the winner. May God save you from such shakers.

ICY COLD SHAKE

Have you ever shaken hands with a person who was all-smiles but his hand was as cool as ice. My theory for such handshakes and such people is that they are cold-blooded manipulators and self-centred narcissists. They won't hesitate a second while backstabbing and backbiting you if it helps their cause. Be careful of such people.

WARM WELCOME

If the hand feels comfortably warm, solid grip, healthy grasp and slight movement, it is the sign of a mature firm handshake. And since I think of myself as the one who offers such a handshake, I may be biased in terming this as the best handshake.

So let us shake hands for a healthy relationship.

~ ~ ~

CHAPTER 26

Affectation Effect

A big company was going through a crisis and a new CEO joined at this crucial juncture to turn around the company. He took the unions head on and opened direct channels of communication with the employees. Company was incurring financial losses. At such a time, CEO encouraged expenses on song, dance, drama programmes. He took strong punitive actions against union members but he himself could be seen in clubs in the evenings enjoying drinks. People started questioning his ways and doubting his intentions. After 3 years, company began making profits. So people wanted to understand his ways. He told them that when he joined the company, town life was almost dead. People had pre-judged the fate of the company and the whole town had starting behaving as if it was dead already. He wanted to bring back life to the town. That is why even in financial crunch, he allowed expenses on reviving the cultural activities. So that people could start enjoying life and become hopeful. As for club evenings, he explained that while the confrontation with union was going on, chances were that people would have taken him to be against employees of the company. By going to club and meeting all levels of employees and mingling with them, he wanted to give the message that all is well and good days will come back soon. If people see CEO getting worried and stressed, it would have sent a wrong message. That his affectations with a purpose worked was evident from results of the company. And that is what I am calling as affectation effect.

In India, under the new government, lot of things are happening. Some things are being labelled as drama, show-off etc. Even I myself thought of some things as superficial. But on deeper analysis, I found that silent action is going on, but it is being supported by drama as affectation works, whether it be a company or a country. Youth energy is being channelised to positive thoughts and actions. Causes are being generated to drive positive mindset and collective change. Let us see who has the last laugh here.

Affectation effect can also be seen in our relationship with our seniors and elders. They at times act strong deliberately to mend our ways. An angry boss, a strict parent, a hard taskmaster and a disciplinarian, are all examples of such behaviour. This may be for self-interest at times on their part, but affectation works here too.

What say?

~ ~ ~

CHAPTER 27
Apologize anyway

"You are not God, just another screwed-up human being. Let yourself feel better, so that you can keep yourself feeling better. Apologize, don't try to fix what you can't, just move on." This was told to Dr. House by Dr. Nolan in the TV series House, MD. What Doctor House had done was to reinforce the thoughts of a mentally disturbed person that latter had super powers. So the poor guy jumped from a high rise and almost died. Dr. House was feeling guilty but did not want to apologize as he thought apology for such a huge mistake was useless and superficial. What was done could not be undone. Then Dr. Noaln told him this.

Now don't we all face similar situations one time or the other? When we goof up, hurt someone and then go to our cocoons. We want to make up but think that plain sorry is not enough. So we don't even do that. An irony indeed.

At other times, we feel that the other person is at fault and not us. So we let a relation and friendship rot and self-destruct. Boss, that is why the dispute arose because we differed. So let us talk it out in such situations, agree to disagree and move on.

Believe you me, apology is a great sweetener and softener. Because it has become a rarity, it is welcomed as and when it is tendered. Well, most of the times. If you have committed some lapse at office and senior is angry, just say sorry from the heart, and see things cool down in a jiffy. I have seen people feeling guilty at once, if someone says sorry. Because they realize it's not that big a thing after all that they are shouting and screaming at. But for sorry to matter, let it be used pragmatically, and not on every small sneeze.

Of course sorry has to be genuine and should appear so. And to a junior it will sound like sweet music, if a heartfelt apology comes from a senior when it is needed. We all love extinct things.

At times, some people are rigid and don't respond to your apology. Even then at least you have done your part in maintaining a relationship, rest is upto the other person. And there is a limit to what you can do after all.

But I can assure you that most of the times, saying a sincere sorry and meaning it, will resolve many issues.

So even when you feel that the other person is equally or more at fault, you take the lead and apologize anyway.

~ ~ ~

CHAPTER 28

Smile It Away

Someone has said "I don't smile because I am happy, I am happy because I smile." How true. Smile does bring about a subtle, subconscious change in attitude of the one who smiles and the ones who are smiled at. Now every smile may not be categorised as disarming smile. But the element of disarming is inherent in every smile. If someone is coming to you with the intention of arguing with you, and you welcome him with a smile, half his anger will vapourise.

Then there are times when someone makes an irritating comment or acts in a way that makes you angry. At those times, best strategy to adopt is to just smile it away. Because most of the times, it's all momentary. Reacting in any other way or making a nasty remark is not going to help in any way other than to complicate the things.

There are times when people exceed their briefs and start offering advice without being asked for. Just smile instead of snubbing them, saves lots of angry moments. Then there are occasions when role clarity, role overlapping, reverse delegation, role reversal or role confusion incidents take place at work, just smile and move on. Saves lot of heartburn. At times, your politeness is taken as submissiveness and people tend to take you for granted. A meaningful smile at these times can serve the dual purpose of conveying your disapproval and keep things calm.

So, just smile it away.

~ ~ ~

CHAPTER 29
Perfection virus

Well, first of all, let me tell you, I am not a perfectionist by any stretch of imagination. Perfection I am talking of is in others, which is a pain in the neck when you are at the receiving end, and the expectation of perfection that we have from others which causes unnecessary stress.

First, the perfectionists- genuine or pseudo (knowingly or unknowingly). Perfectionists as bosses are really very dangerous. If you end up with such a boss, be prepared for 100 revisions of every draft, 500 rehearsals of every event, nit-picking, shouting/ snide remarks depending on his temperament, delays in projects, every situation turning into a crisis, worst time management, avoidable tantrums, the list goes on. You can't understand the severity of the problem unless you have faced it yourself.

Coming to the expectation part. Well this is basically to do with stress management. We tend to have expectations of perfection from our seniors and juniors. Why is my boss not caring enough, why does she not understand I have personal problems too, why is she so demanding, why can't she be accommodating and understanding like other bosses (grass is always greener principle), why my hard work is not recognized, why-why-why. Well, no one is perfect, not us, not our bosses. Each person has strengths and weaknesses. As do our juniors. We expect them to behave like an ideal junior. He should listen to and do everything I say, he should not insubordinate, he should reciprocate my professionalism, he should be a perfect team member, he should not take my assent for granted, he should respect the age and grade difference, he should be understanding of my going out of the way for maintaining calm and camaraderie by swallowing my pride and ego as a senior, he should not dishonor the mutual trust and personal rapport when it comes to office matters. But then who said world is ideal.

So yours truly has come to the conclusion that for my mental peace and stress free mind, I should accept the seniors and juniors as they are. With juniors, you can try and play the role of a mentor once or twice for each unacceptable behavior, but after that there is really no point in sulking and expecting better from an intelligent professional. You can let go after that. There is no point in wasting your time and energy again and again. Not that I can do much about it, but every time, the unexpected behavior is repeated, it is better to ignore and go on. As they say, if you can't change others, change yourself. There is no point in trying to infuse my view of an ideal senior or junior on colleagues. Each person comes as a package, and I should take it in my stride. There are good things in every person, I should try and enjoy them. As far as bad things, in my view at least, better way is to close your eyes and bless that person. That way I can practice modern nirvana and attain peace of mind, my first and foremost priority.

~ ~ ~

CHAPTER 30
Telesales tales

The other day, I missed a call from some unknown cell number. When I called back later saying I missed a call from this number, the reply I got was a classic. It was a call from some telesales company, which in itself is irritating. You can ignore land lines, but cell numbers you tend to call back, thinking that it might be an important number. Anyway, so this lady who picked up when I called back, says- I don't really know, I have been calling many people, so which Sanjay, I can't say. What a tele caller.

She could have responded smartly and said, "Yes Sir, I am from XYZ company and I had called for this purpose. Would you be interested.?" But she ended up acting foolish. But maybe fault is not hers, but her employer's. They did not train her properly for all such situations.

One another frequent problem I face from them is rudeness. Now I consider myself a polite talker, so when I get such a call, I say in a nice tone, no thanks and then add- Have a good day. But most often what I get back is-

Why not?

Hear me out first?

My boss will talk to you?

And best response to my - have a good day- is banging of phone at their end. If I am not interested in their product, I can go screw myself, they are least bothered. So no ok sir, no you too, no no issues, Just a BANG. Wow, what customer service.

Have you tried calling the call-centres? You must have. I will skip the 1000-option menu, and tell about the customer service executive. Most of the times, they end up not solving the problem and to rub salt on the wound, their parting question is- Is there anything else I can help you with? @#$%^&*(*&$# you did not help with what I called for, and you are asking me anything else. Other standard responses are

Sorry sir, server is not working, call back after 15 minutes. (and waste 5 minutes on menu again)

Sorry sir, this is our company policy? (then a machine can do your job, dumbo, take feedback and assure)

No sir, I can not transfer your call, you will have to call again for technical/customer support team? (How do I understand your definitions of technical and customer support, if you both keep shuttling me)

And while we are at phone etiquette, my three pet peeves

- People putting you on speakerphone at their end, without telling you

- People munching things while they are talking over phone (it really resounds in the ear)

- People coming to you and starting talking, when they can see you are on a call and speaking to someone.

Your peeves?

~ ~ ~

CHAPTER 31

Noisy Silence

"Employees will interpret the manager's silence through their own points of view, based on their backgrounds, experiences, and the types of relationships they have with their manager." (NR Carroll)

While reading these lines, I was reminded of many instances from last 20 odd years of my work life, when silence created situations. Though I am a firm believer of the adage, silence is wisdom and if you are silent, you cannot be misquoted. But there is the other side of the coin for sure.

I tried to follow a need-to-know policy with my team and assigned tasks as per job profiles. But this selective silence was not liked by some and they blamed me for favouring some at the cost of others.

I reciprocated the respect and cooperation I received from 1-2 juniors and I was blamed for cosying up to them since they were seen as high-fliers and were close to higher-ups.

I tried to give space to colleagues and gave them freedom to work at their own pace and in their own style. I was blamed for being too detached and stoic.

Arrogant and indifferent are also adjectives not unfamiliar to me.

I try to maintain a low profile and don't beat drums about what I did, rather I give credit to my team. What this led to is that one of my reporting bosses in the past complained to department head and said, what does sanjay do the whole day? That is what silence can do. Anyways the head told me, and I was like what the heck. I wanted to barge into his room and shout. But I controlled myself because boss would know that the head told me. I needed to take criticism in stride and learn about the true character of people. If I raised the issue, the head will not trust me and even other people will not tell things to me in future. But I learnt a valuable lesson about noisy silence.

What about you?

~ ~ ~

CHAPTER 32
Analysis-paralysis or Haste-makes-waste

Going by the speed at which new decisions and announcements are being made these days set me thinking of the dilemma I faced few months back.

Actually I am one of those personality types who first think of plan-b before starting a new project. I was lucky that my immediate senior had the philosophy of saying no to any new thing. So by comparison my approach seemed docile and accommodating. I always say to whoever is ready to hear that tasks succeed when there is 60 % planning and 40 % executing. But in reality it is 20 % planning and 80 % executing. Deadlines are preponed at whims and fancies, commitments are given without proper groundwork.

So I was more inclined to tilt towards analysis-paralysis, as in my view, being cautious and well-prepared results in better outcome. I have been snubbed in some meetings for being the if-and-but guy, and for being pessimistic and over-analytical. But there is a brighter side too, when at times, CEOs and Directors have appreciated my ideas and notings in writing.

To give one example, we wanted to reduce the cost of advertising in our company. But no PSU had worked on the lines we were planning to. We wanted to reduce the agency commission substantially and also wanted them to do designing and release of tender and other ads. Our Head of Department(HOD) gave free hand. So I invited top media buying agencies, understood the working and organised meetings with HOD. After 6 months of consultations and planning, we floated the tender and chose one agency, and got savings of around 10 times in the agency commission that we were paying. Perhaps we were the first PSU to do so in the country. Many people cribbed and ranted. But since the process was transparent, it got substantial recurring savings and was assessed as valid and rational. So it was seemingly an analysis-paralysis case, but the time spent resulted in accomplishment of a big task.

I was basking in my glory, when a jolt brought me back to reality. A new boss had come and he wanted to take our company onto new media. He discussed with our team, and I was my defensive self as usual. I said, we are a B2B company, so we really need to understand the Ws and Hs first. He did not say anything at that time. But after some days I saw that our company had forayed into new media. Boss had assigned the task to my reportee directly and this reportee was doing her best to make a noise. I won't go into the final result of that initiative as

I may sound biased. But here my view of haste-makes-waste was resulting in me being side lined. A junior was assigned the task, I was branded as a nay-sayer and a doubting Thomas.

This incident got me thinking which is the right approach, taking your time to plan and then execute. Or go with the flow, start the new job and improvise as the job progresses. Don't tell me middle way is the best way.

Which side are you on? hasty tasty or slow and steady.

~ ~ ~

CHAPTER 33
COOCZ

Well this was the acronym I had developed for dealing with a stressful situation at work. We had a new boss and she used to give different new assignments, which I was not very comfortable with. I had usual fear of unknown, was not sure of myself and I did not want to be branded as a failure. My situation was complicated because of the fact that in the past if something wrong happened, I was chosen as the scapegoat. One boss had gone to the extent of asking me to draft the warning letter that was to be issued to me. Out of decency, I never dared to tell my bosses that you checked the whole thing, you were overseeing it, you even made changes in some portions and now you are putting the entire blame on me. Then again because of my so-called leadership principles, I never blamed my juniors for any mistake by our team. As a leader I used to take the blame on me. So I expected the same from my bosses, which did not happen with one particular boss. Other bosses including this lady boss provided full cover though.

Anyways coming back to my fear of new assignments. I thought to myself, what is the worst that could happen.

I would fail. But then everyone knows I am not heading a department, job is new, so my failure, if it happens, will be forgiven. But if after 10 years, I head some department and then I don't have any clue of how the job is to be done, that will be ten times the embarrassment. So better to face my fears now. Better to come out of my shell and cocoon now. At least, I have a chance of learning a new thing. So instead of blaming the boss for dumping new jobs on me, I should take it as an opportunity to learn new jobs and maybe prove my potential there too. I had to the do the job anyhow since boss has assigned it. So what is the point of sulking and cribbing.

That is when I came out with this saying for myself- COOCZ. Any guesses?

Well, it's come-out-of-comfort-zone.

~ ~ ~

CHAPTER 34
Life is People

Jim Collins, in an interview shared that these are the three words (life is People) he and his wife use as a philosophy of life. How true. He explained this with a simple example. He used to go rock-climbing and planned beforehand which rocks/hills he wants to go for. But after adopting this philosophy of Life is People, he now decides who all he wants to go rock-climbing with, and then choosing rocks/hills.

As they say things easiest to understand are difficult to practice. Let me share my personal experience in this regard.

I don't feel like arguing or fighting with a colleague, thinking that we have to work together and after heated arguments, it becomes difficult to work normally. I succeed in doing this most of the times, but once or twice in a year, I lose my temper and raise my voice. At times I realize the mistake soon enough and apologize to the other person, but at times situation becomes complicated. Then comes an agonizing phase when working with that person for next few days becomes a punishment. At those times, if I can remind myself that Life-is-people, maybe I can control my anger.

At times, seniors start taking you for granted and play with you and your emotions like a toy. At such times, I am never sure about the origin of my meekness. Is it my non-assertiveness, my please-all mentality or my don't-burn-the-bridges attitude. Whatever the case maybe, in such cases, the burden of internalizing Life-is-People principle applies on seniors, who treat people like pawns in a game of chess. Don't know if I will ever have the guts to call a spade a spade. But before that I need to find out the cause of my cowardice. Search is on.

Coming to juniors, I have always prided myself on being a humane and caring team-leader. At times, being such a Life-is-People boss is a real pain, as one has to adjust to the tantrums, drama, insubordination, neglect, carelessness, moodiness, ambitions and laziness of team-members. But some of these behaviours maybe fragments of my imagination. Most of the times, it's emotionally draining for me as I am yet to achieve a Buddha state of mind. But here, I stick to my life-is-people principle 100 per cent. At least I think so.

But I can't say the same about situations outside work, say relations. Most of the relatives come with a baggage of past incidences with them or their families. We start seeing them with those goggles. I must confess I am not that much accommodating to my relatives, as I am to my juniors. Maybe because I am selfish and I have to work with the team every day. But still even in family relations, we need to be less biased, less prejudiced and more open. Why? Because life-is-people.

I may sound pedantic, but for attaining such a state-of-mind, we need to get rid of our ego, selfishness, self-centredness, anger, jealousy, greed and other such vices.

Aim for the moon.......

~ ~ ~

CHAPTER 35

Crowd Mentality

The other day, I had a bad experience. I was travelling by Delhi metro train and was to get down at CS station. But the crowd waiting outside at the station, to get inside the train, pushed me back inside and ran in, like a group of mad sheep. I tried my level best to squeeze and wriggle out but I could not. And the doors closed. I was obviously angry. And I heard people making snide and sadistic remarks- Poor guy, could not get out etc. Suddenly some wisecrack made a comment on how I should be ready to move out. That blew my fuse.

This was a crowd of 50-60 people, who were all white-collared employees, supposedly graduate professionals or college-going students. And they foolishly became a part of the crowd and rushed in like mad bulls. Since the train seats were already filled, so none of them was running in for a seat. They were running in for a place to stand in the train. They knew very well that a person is not able to get down due to their foolishness but none of them showed the decency to give me way. They were like blind-folded donkeys. Then some of these guys were so arrogant that they decided to laugh at the victim and made funny remarks. Now they vs. I, for me it was an avoidable extra travel, time, money and irritation. After I got trapped inside by their foolishness and crowd mentality, I had no choice but to suffer all these things. For each one of them, it was a matter of waiting for 2 more minutes for the next train. But these bunch of idiots chose to play sheep and made me suffer.

I know this is a small incident and I am over-reacting, but what this made me think of was, how crowds and mobs go mad and do silly, stupid things.

I was facing a group of 50 people, and the sheer physical force they created was impossible to counter. I was extrapolating the situation to an angry mob and I could understand their psyche and actions. If literate, educated and white-collared guys whose only motivation was to get inside the train first could be so maddening. Imagine a crowd of illiterate, angry and misinformed people, who are misled by a supposedly greater motivation like religion, race, educational benefit, reservation and what not.

Can you really blame them for behaving the way they do. So this small mishap made me see the workings of crowd mentality.

~ ~ ~

CHAPTER 36

Management, *Karma* and *The Gita*

Every time I read something on Management learnings from The Bhagavad Gita, I used to be confused as to how a book written hundreds of years ago on non-management issues could be relevant for managers. This was until I attended a lecture by Swami Sukhbodhananda. He pointed out how The Gita is a manual on management of emotional crisis. Whatever crises we face at work in today's times are not in any way more severe than the one Arjuna faced viz. killing his blood relations in a war. And throughout the 18 chapters of the book, Lord Krishna, the master gives him tips to overcome the crisis and face the problem head-on. Could there be more valid reason for reading the book and learning management lessons.

One other thing that always bothered me was how Krishna is lecturing Arjuna in the middle of battlefield and all other warriors on both sides are waiting for the lecture to finish before starting the war. This question of mine was also answered by Swami's lecture. He pointed out that we presume Krishna and Arjuna talking in the same way that we talk. Reality is not like that. In fact, both of them talked on a different plain and frame of reference. They talked at a different wavelength and on a level of mind which we cannot even imagine and relate to. Krishna would have conveyed the whole Gita in a jiffy.

Now coming to the concept of Karma, the most confusing shloka I found is No. 47 in Chapter-2. The reason being that the verse suggests - Your right is to work only, but never to the fruit thereof. Now in a world where people want fruit without doing any work, how could one not claim right to the fruit of work done. Some interpretations suggest that expecting fruit is kool, but being attached to the fruit is not. Now, now. You can't have it both ways. If you expect, and you don't get, you will be disappointed, attached or not attached. And if you don't expect any fruit means you don't have a goal. How can that be. Even if you don't expect any monetary or tangible fruit, and you want the results that again is a form of fruit.

So till I get a good explanation from you or find it myself, the question hangs in the air.

~ ~ ~

CHAPTER 37
Things small but significant

The other day, I went to a McD outlet and ordered a soft serve. The guy was supposed to return some change to me and he did that by throwing the coin on the counter. I objected to it and pointed out that you don't throw money like that, I am not a beggar. Another customer waiting in the queue nodded and quipped- Because he is doing that, he is here. Meaning that if he had better manners and attitude of customer service, he would have gone places.

It was a very small incident, but it reminded me of another similar incident in the past. Our landlord's son wanted to borrow some money. So he and his wife came to us and chit-chatted for long before coming to the point. Since we had some sparable money, we gave it to them. After few weeks, they called us to their home for a cup of tea. And that @#$%^ guy came and threw the bundle of money on the table and said here is your money. To add insult to injury, he added- We had money with us, but we did not want to break our fixed-deposit midway, so we asked from you. #$%^&*. Hope you get what I mean.

Moving on from McD customer service to malls, in most of the big shopping chain stores, I come across sales staff which is more interested in himself than in customer. Small things like giving way to customer is alien to them. Customer service is not in their temperament. That is why one feels pity at them. They would rather stand in corner in groups and chat among themselves, than serving the customer. Such is their attitude.

That brings me to another small but funny incident. A friend gifted me a book on my birthday. But I got to know that he had first read that same copy (meaning used it before gifting), then got it gift-wrapped and gifted to me. I am not sure if it was bought for me, or was a pass-it-on. But it did hurt me as I was gifted a used thing. A confession here, after I overcame my hurt, the idea started appealing to me and I thought of doing the same to others. But I could not bring myself up to do that, as once or twice I planned that, I felt like being unfair and impersonal.

So small things whether in personal or professional life, do matter.

~ ~ ~

CHAPTER 38

Go, get a Goal

This one I wrote for my young friends. We are not going to talk about tongue-twisters or alliteration, though the title might mislead you into believing that. We are talking philosophy of life here, so be serious. And coming from a person like me who rarely stuck to a life-goal for more than a couple of days, it should mean something, right! Coz I've learnt it the hard way.

Actually when asked what I wanted to do with my life, my standard answer used to be "Well, as of now, I plan to be a writer (or doctor, engineer, singer.. the list is endless)". What all this meant was that I could not prioritize my life-schedule, and it was through sheer luck that I could get a respectable job, at least to me it appears respectable.

Focus then is the key-word here.

I am not asking you to follow Arjuna of Mahabharata though (you of course can, if you want to), coz then you will curse me later for advising you to forgo other pleasures of life and concentrating only on studies/ career.

That is not me. I am all in for enjoying life at all ages, in all its hues. Specially when you are young, you need to have *full fun*. No financial responsibility, no family to support, no pretensions for social gatherings and so on. I would have been envious of you, had I not been aware of other international tensions you people have at your age. Well, still it is your time, guys. Have fun on the run.

But, yes the Almighty BUT, is that this is also the age and time when you can make or break your career. If you take an overdose of the fun part and neglect the serious part, only you are to blame. It IS your life, isn't it? So if you decide to squander away the precious life-shaping years, don't ask me who was at fault. Then merely doing your course-work and getting good grades is not enough.

You need to think, think and think, what you want to be in life. That is why I asked you to go and get a goal. "My friend is doing Bio, so me too", "That college has a hep crowd, so I'll go there" and " Papa wants me to be an engineer, though I hate Physics, Chemistry", are all life-spoiling statements.

You and only you know what you are good at, what you like doing the most, and where do you see yourself, say ten years from now. If you don't, then take the trouble of knowing it by asking yourself these questions again and again. What makes you happy, is the critical point. Is it money (don't be ashamed if it does, you have got company), peace of mind, helping others, solving challenging or technical problems, creative writing or making computer programs. Think seriously and decide, coz if you want your adrenalin flowing day-in and day-out, choose a career of your liking and then start working towards making that career possible and fulfilling your dreams.

Day dreams with a pinch of realism are more likely to be realized.

~ ~ ~

CHAPTER 39
Appraisal Paradoxes

I always find it very tricky to assess the performance and potential of juniors.

In most organisations, we have a standard form with set criteria on which to assess an individual. But then what of the personaility types of the assessee and assessor, e.g. if I am a person who always wants to hog limelight, I would not like an overambitious junior. But if I like to put ambitious nature of my junior to good use by giving him opportunities to shine, then I won't mind having such a junior. If I am a hypocrite and I don't mind backbiting rather I enjoy it, I won't see anything bad if a junior behaves the same way because that appears natural to me. However if I am a person who prefers straight talk, then I would not like a double-faced junior much. If I am non-assertive, I can rate an assertive junior in two ways. Either I like him because he is exact opposite of me and can be complementary in team, or I can hate his guts and rate him lower. It's all very subjective.

Secondly, I won't like to rate very low, even my least performing junior because I know that in other departments there are people worse than him who get rated 98-99. So why should my team member suffer. But I can't rate all my team members 99-100, because then that will be injustice to good performers. It's all very very confusing.

I remember in my last performance appraisal meeting, one of my juniors told me, you don't utilize the skills and talent of your juniors fully. And irony is that as and when I give some responsible job to that junior, I end up cleaning up the mess. He is good attitude-wise, rather the best, but when it comes to tasks, he screws up or needs 100 reminders.

Then comes the question of young team members, millennials if you like. They have peculiar working styles. They may not work for 4 hours at a stretch, keep doing web surfing in office time, but when it comes to crisis management, or working from home on urgent assignments they don't bat an eyelid, and get going. How does one assess them. Then there are those who stick to 9 to 5 deadline most of the time, need their extended lunch breaks, but are so good at whatever they do and so sincere that you tend to ignore their officiousness. Some however are easy to assess, who prefer to do the least, take maximum possible time to do a job, never-say-no but never-do-it-either types. They will get a straight 95 from me. Rest I will have to juggle between 96 and 99. I am yet to find a perfect 100.

And I am thinking of developing my own assessment sheet based on my needs and requirements.

~ ~ ~

CHAPTER 40
Crude lessons from Rude people

The other day I had to talk to a senior in our company about some official work. I called on his phone and briefed him. But he was very curt, dismissive and bossy in his tone. Though I had heard things about him, I thought of him to be a nice person. So yesterday's talk opened my eyes. **I realized that I had been talking in a similar manner to some of my colleagues when they were being pushy or unreasonable in my view. After yesterday, I have resolved that I shall try to be more courteous, accommodating and polite with my colleagues.**

A few days back, I gave a small job to one of our agencies, because the agency was getting a similar job done the same day so I thought of piggybacking this small job. But that guy called and asked why are you giving this small time job, we are not a photocopy shop. I was shocked but later **I realized that other people/agencies, which were polite, might also be thinking in a similar manner and might not be telling me. So I resolved to be cautious in future.**

A former big boss was known for his rash and angry nature. Once I had to show preview of a corporate film to him with my boss. He saw it, suggested some changes and asked us to show it again next day. While editing, I noticed that one of his suggestions was not looking okay visually, so I changed a bit. Next day when he saw the film he was furious and shouted, "If you have to do your own thing, why are you wasting my time?" I said sorry and later felt sorry also. He was right in his own way. **Though later he did agree to my point of view but he made me realize that we should not take big boss›s time for granted.**

Then there was this girl from a newspaper marketing wing. I am usually proud of my forthrightness and honesty. So I told her that we will not release tenders to her newspaper as the profile did not fit our requirement. She started arguing with me, gave me reasons and countered my view logically. I did not like it at first but then later **I realized she was acting very professionally and was right in fighting for ads to her newspapers. Other persons from different newspapers nodded to whatever I said and I got trapped in my superiority complex. But here was this girl who showed me the other side of the coin.**

Then there is this motor-mouth colleague in our building who keeps commenting on things personal and official. She once commented on my shabby cubicle, and **as usual I disliked her for that. But later on I realized that she was right.** I needed to clean my cubicle which I did eventually.

So rude people can teach us a lot if we think objectively and analyse what they said on our face. **Polite people will adjust to our faults, not rude people.** And that to me is the positive side of rudeness.

~ ~ ~

CHAPTER 41

Boss-isms

I have worked with many bosses in my 23 years of working experience. Each boss has some good and some bad habits. But bad habit in a boss irritates like anything, as does in a spouse. Reason being that we have to live and work with them on a daily basis, and both have a kind of control on us, i daresay. I have tried to list these bad habits here which I observed in my bosses and which I think, just think, that I don't have them as a boss.

1- Making fun of you in front of colleagues.

2- Talking to you while he can clearly see you are on phone.

3- Disturbing you at lunch time.

4- Calling you at odd hours and Shouting at you.

5- Putting the entire blame for a mistake on you, when he was very much part of the decision making process.

6- Not bothering about your personal problems as long as his selfish interest is served.

7- Sharing confidential things about you in public, which he got to know from you or elsewhere.

8- Backstabbing and backbiting you, specially before your juniors. Divide-and-rule policy.

9- Expecting that you suck up to him whether he deserves any respect or not.

10- Recalling a personal help he did once, hundred times over.

11- Usurping common office (pool) facilities using seniority by making you wait and then going around the town claiming he is the fastest.

12- Grabbing full credit for things he did not do at all.

13- Not sharing with you the reasons for chaging your role or profile.

14- Expecting you to do his personal errands.

15- Tagging you along in parties and functions just for his ego.

16- Expecting you to do menial jobs because he does them.

17- Telling stories of how things were differnt in his times when he was junior and used to handle whole organisation.

18- When you hesitate in accepting a job, trying to blackmail you by saying ok i will do it.

19- Giving all the benefits to other peers and depriving you of all. (Okay, this may be subjective)

20- Assigning jobs to your team, without even informing you, and then expecting feedback from you on these jobs.

21- Depriving you of trainings, workshops and vacations saying you are indispensable. Work will suffer. BS.

22- Never ever thinking about your motivation.

23- Listening to only those people who shout back or react.

Enough for today, rest some other day.

You are welcome to add to the list.

(Views expressed here are personal, have deliberately excluded experiences with present bosses for selfish reasons)

~ ~ ~

CHAPTER 42

Dilemmas at Work

I have seen many seniors and juniors playing all sort of tricks to get credit for a work, which they did only partially or just supervised. It feels strange to me. But I know that this would appear normal and justified to people who are credit-grabbers. My personal view is that if you give credit to your team members whether in front of them or in their absence, the credit indirectly comes to you because if your team is performing well, means you are managing and leading well.

However if I try to give credit to my boss in front of him, it almost always seems like sucking up to him. So I have stopped doing that. Moreover one of my bosses in previous job had this habit of praising a junior for a job well done, and when the junior accepted it with grace or with arrogance, boss started criticizing him the moment the junior went out. Boss said, "What has he done, all work I did and he is gladly accepting the credit." I always thought that she must be doing the same to me. So I got doubly cautious with her.

One another thing which has me confused is the relation between my boss and my juniors. As a practice,

I encouraged them to go to boss and update him on the ongoing jobs. My feeling is that this way they get motivated and feel happy to talk to Head of Department, and also get to know that I am not after credit for jobs they do. But the flip side to this is that at times I get the feeling that boss thinks of me as one arrogant junior who ignores/neglects him and sends juniors to him. Paradox indeed. Today only, I was given a task by a senior and since another colleague had worked on related task a day before I asked him to do the task and explained what is required. Within minutes, this colleague calls up boss and asks the details of the task in front of me. What is to be done, how it is to be done. I had explained all this to him. I was shocked, to say the least, to see how to earn brownie points, this colleague totally undermined my role. He acted as if I had not explained the task to him and almost proved me incompetent in front of the boss. And to add salt to injury, this was done in front of me. This made me think on how many earlier occasions, this colleague and others have gone and done this on my back, without me knowing, and god knows with how many seniors. So note to myself, try to do most of the work assigned to you yourself, if possible. Team is indeed over-rated.

One another dilemma I faced many a times is the late-sitting thing. I used to think that late sitting is my choice and the only negative effect is on my family time. However I read an article in HBR that this alienates other colleagues from me, who feel that I am spoiling their image by comparison, since they go out in time. Office-office, what to do.

Let me conclude this post with a quote I read somewhere, always work hard, because competition is less in this field of hard workers, compared to people who want to grab credit.

~ ~ ~

CHAPTER 43
Never mix personal & official relations

Having burnt my fingers several times, by doing what I am advising against, makes me a perfect example for learning from my experiences as to what not to do. You can start by calling me a fool. As they say, if you make a mistake once it's okay and if you make the same mistake twice, problem is with you. This is because second time it's not a mistake but a choice.

I won't bore you with all my follies in this area, but just share two examples.

One is of a senior with whom I worked 10 years back. He was the epitome of narcissism, selfishness and arrogance. Everyone used to say about him that he is very nice as a person, however he maybe a pain as a manager. I got duped and trusted him with my personal feelings and views. That proved to be my biggest mistake. He used all those personal details against me as and when required. If he had helped me at some time in the past, he made me realize that 100 times in the future. Every time I asked for a transfer to my hometown, he threw my family situation on my face in front of my seniors. Basically whatever I shared with him as a supposedly family-friend I thought him to be, he shared with one and all in office. After that incident, I had made it a policy of never to make family friends with seniors. Other reason for that is most seniors (barring a few exceptions I know) always think of such personal gestures to be sucking-up-gesture. So even if your intentions are good, genuine and sincere, in all likelihood, you will be stamped as boot licker. Of course there are some good souls who recognise and appreciate such gestures to be what they are. But such people can be counted on finger tips. So I prefer giving thanks to and having festival meet-ups with people who are no longer in a position to advance my career in any way. That goes against the so-called rules of networking but is something that does not go against the grain. My life vision being-Peace of mind.

Second incident is with a junior I worked in my previous job. I covered up her goof-ups and shared blame with her, I ignored her basic repetitive mistakes and carelessness in translations thinking she will learn with time, I graded her at par with others so that she is not disheartened, I adjusted to her mood tantrums and forgave mistakes, lapses as she was going through a tough phase in life and I accepted her disobedience and insubordination at times for the same reason. This is not all, she used to call me at midnight to share personal problems, at times she used to come to our home and we (me and wife) counselled her till 1 and 2 in the night.

At times I stayed back in office and took care of her work, so that she could attend to personal work. I know I did all this on my own, and it was my decision.

But what do I get in return. She starts shouting at me for her appraisal ratings that our seniors decided. I supported her and went with her to senior. Then she calls me at 10 in the night on a weekend when I am having dinner. I take the call anyway and try to console her. She says, she is very stressed, I try to convince her that promotion should not be a problem. She still maintains loud tone and disrespectful tone, and when I ask her, she calls me unfair, biased and judgmental. I stop giving work to her and forgetting all that I had done for her, she goes to my boss and bitches against me.

Then she comes to apologize and says, you are unfair, biased and judgmental but I am sorry. She is not even able to understand that I can accept loud tone, even bitching to boss, but the fact that after what all I did for her, she can assume I can be judgmental towards her, is unforgivable.

So guys, learn from my mistakes and never mix personal and official relations.

~ ~ ~

CHAPTER 44

Managing Sportively

One often hears that team-working in offices can be effective, if every team member works with a sportsman spirit. Yours truly took this statement a bit too literally and mused on what sort of teams and team-members one could visualise in an office environment. Here is a sample of what my weird mind churned out.

Tennis Players: They never keep the ball in their court. The buck should never stop at their place. They either pass it on to their seniors (upward delegation?) or juniors. The analogy seems more apt in Table-tennis, with files/notes/memos etc. moving to and fro on tables, just like the ball.

Kabaddi (an Indian game, with one person wrestling with many in opposing team) Players: They keep on repeating 'I-me-myself' till they are exhausted and are breathless, and then their game is lost. They give their Egos, euphemistic names like self-confidence, self-esteem, assertiveness and so on. They presume that everyone else, adept at using his emotional intelligence, is taking part in a popularity contest.

Hockey Players: They always keep a stick in their hands, never a carrot. Seems like they never heard of the carrot-and-stick policy. Though Covey also, in his 'The 8th Habit' would have us believe that this policy is for animals, and we should give more stress on Conscience, or SQ as he calls it.

Athletes: They are always in a hurry, no matter what. Most of the times, these look-busy-do-nothing types keep running away from the goal. Problem is that they keep on running even when the race is over. No wonder they are never in line with their team.

Cheer-leaders: They sit on the fence and keep cheering and cheering and cheering, always a source of motivation and inspiration through their lectures. For a change, they never do anything though.

Chess Players: You are either a pawn or a competitor for them. Choose whatever you like,

Football players: I can only pray for you that you do not get to work with such guys. Three or four of them can be a deadly combination, using you as a football. You complete a letter given by one boss, and the other calls you for the next assignment. You haven't yet finished it and the buzzer rings telling you that the boss's boss wants to discuss some IR problem with you and so on and on....

Squash Players: May God save their team-mates, especially if they are within the firing range of these anger-freaks. One never gets to know with them why one is getting the beating. Others are to blame for their every problem-personal or official, and the only outlet they know is to give a piece, a really big one, of their minds to others whenever they are upset. And they are upset a lot.

Umpires: How could one forget cricket in the country of Tendulkars and Sehwags. Well, the umpires are prone to giving their opinion on each and every matter, needless to say without the same being sought for. And strangely, their views are brimming with negativity. They know what PM, CM, Chairman or a mere colleague should have done in different situations. As someone rightly pointed out, the solutions to all the problems being faced by the country and the world are known only to rickshaw-pullers and hair-dressers. Alas, they are where they are!

So this was what I meant by Managing Sportively. Well, in the end you must be wondering in which category of players do I place myself. To be frank, and without any traces of modesty, yours truly can boast of himself as a jack-of-all and an all-rounder.

~ ~ ~

CHAPTER 45
Management Panchatantra

'Slow and Steady wins the race' is not the only management lesson that we can learn from the Animal Kingdom. Just as we realize the significance of Perseverance through the hare and **tortoise** story, we can add to our repertoire by observing other animals too. Whether it be planning, discipline, team-working, dedication to the job or any other management concept, Vishnu Sharma's (of Panchatantra fame) Training Academy viz. The Animal Kingdom, has ample practitioners who believe in deeds rather than mere words alone.

Take **Ants** for example. These tiny creatures are the best known Planners in animal-kind. You may get irritated by rows and rows of ants on your walls and floors, but the ants don't bother, because they know their priorities. They are actually taking their ration for storage, which they will use when they can't come out due to adverse weather. Another remarkable thing about ants is that they are Team-workers and are very Goal-oriented. You try putting an obstacle, say ant-killer, in their way and they will take an alternative route to reach their destination or goal. Such Commitment to the goal is indeed exemplary.

Let's shift gear and learn about the story of an old **Donkey** who became useless for his owner and was thrown into a well. People started throwing dust into the well to bury him alive. End of life for that ill-fated creature? Nope, he had probably heard of the dictum of Converting Challenges to Opportunities or the Stumbling Blocks to Stepping Stones. He kept on stepping up on the mud thrown at him and climbed out of the well to live in freedom and happiness ever after.

The epitome of Loyalty, **Dog**, also has a lesson or two to teach. Other than Pavlov's experiments on Positive and Negative reinforcement, dog exemplifies Alertness and Bravery to fight against all odds.

Self-Discipline, is what we humans can learn from **Cock**. Many of us need to imbibe the habit of living a disciplined life from this early-riser and fierce-fighter.

Chameleon, teaches us to adapt to changing external environment. If only all managers could adapt to the changing business environment as fast as chameleon changes colours to match the external environment, the corporate world would have been a saner, less chaotic place.

The almighty **Lion**, proves by his deeds that to be a great leader, one must do every job with full concentration and vigour i.e. to give 100 per cent to whatever one does.

Whether it be a small hare or the mighty elephant, lion attacks it with full power and ferocity.

In the end, I would like to say that instead of shedding **Crocodile** tears at our workload, or exhibiting **Cat**titude, or having a **Crab** mentality, we should start doing our job and get busy like a **Bee**. And if I may, I would recommend a reading of 'Who moved my cheese' as a beginner's guide to Management Panchatantra.

~ ~ ~

CHAPTER 46
Managing the managers

We come to office to manage, not to make friends. Thus spoke one of my ex-bosses. Well he is not wrong entirely. *We must be as inhuman as possible and treat our team like machine. So what if they have life, family and personal interests.* That is not our concern. If you are willing to practice this unique style of management, here are a few pointers.

Mobile Genie is what your juniors should aim to become. They must pick up your phone in three rings, else they must be ready to face the consequences. That includes the times they are in toilet, bathroom, having meals, at a family function, quarrelling with spouse at home, visiting hospital or cremation ground, having headache or fever. Office comes first, to hell with their lives.

Nirvana should be their mental state. How can a junior even dare to expect credit for a job well done. After all, is it not your able, visionary and ground-breaking leadership that got the job done. Errors and mistakes are ofcourse junior's doing, that is what juniors are for. You must not wait after a crisis to jump on the junior and ensure that whole blame is put on her. Best learning for the junior will happen when he is emotionally upset, sad and beaten down, not when he is in a better frame of mind to analyse the situation after things cool down. You must use I/me/myself at least once in each sentence, when talking of a good team job with HOD, lest they forget your presence.

Whipped cream is the brain composition they must be ready for. You have the birthright to shout at them, abuse them, look down at them, insult them and frown at them. These juniorlings need to be put in place. If you angry, give him a piece of your mind. This does not matter what you are angry for, he better be whip-ready. You didn't shit properly, scold him, you fought with your spouse, scold him, your boss is not happy, scold him, your mood is off, scold him or you are in good mood, scold him. Junior must always be in a liquid state of mind, which is more dynamic and mouldable.

Tail-wagger If junior is able to grow a tail, nothing like that, as he can always wag it as and when required. Second best option is to give him opportunities to show his subservience. Call her when she is having tea, snacks or lunch, start speaking to her ignoring that she is speaking to someone on phone, ignore her in front of other colleagues, throw papers and files at her, cut her in the middle of a sentence while she is speaking, the list is endless. You have to be innovative in your approach.

Pawn is what a junior is. Use him as such. Give same job to three juniors. Overlapping is immaterial, your wish should be their command. Make him revise the draft 36 times, perceived perfection is more important than time management and motivation. Bitching and backbiting are potent tools you can use to make the juniors hate each other. Divide and rule is an approved and tested policy. Make him do menial jobs and errands. He needs to learn how hard life can be. Never tell him how he can improve himself, let him learn by hit and trial. Why should he be benefitting from your hard-earned experience. Let him have his own experience, mentoring is for trainers not bosses.

You can invent your own new ways for managing the managers. Cruelty and heartlessness is the limit.

Let not modesty, kindness, concern, patience be the stumbling blocks in your path to boss-hood.

~ ~ ~

CHAPTER 47

Autonomy, relatedness and competence

An HBR article highlights these three viz. autonomy, relatedness and competence as the three psychological needs, essential for motivation vis-a-vis Maslow's hierarchy of needs.

After reading this article, I introspected and tried to analyse whether lack of these elements led to demotivation for me. And it did.

First, Autonomy. As they say tell me what to do, not how to do it. I fully agree with the necessity of this element. I respect all my ex-bosses who gave me full freedom to work and never micro-managed. Whereas the bosses who were always standing on my neck, looking over mys shoulders and nit-picking never really had a big fan following.

Relatedness. Though I have learnt the hard way that one should never mix personal relations with official relations. But maybe I took the relations to one extreme. And it is not necessary to go overboard to have relatedness. Coming to my bosses, the ones that never really took pains to develop relatedness, appeared more professional, focused, no-nonsense and straightforward. I justified their curtness, bluntness and indifference to others, as a mark of their working style and emphasis on sharing info on need-to-know basis. But to tell you the truth, inspite of all these justifications and explanations, I always felt something missing. That was relatedness.

Lastly, competence. Working in a PSE has its pros and cons. For a knowledge-hungry person like me, it is really challenging. I paid life membership of management bodies like AIMA etc. from my own pocket so that I can enrich myself by attending seminars and conferences. I subscribed to magazines like HBR etc. for keeping myself abreast with latest development and thinking in management. I devote 1-2 hours a day on internet for this purpose. I only wish.... somethings are better left unsaid.

~ ~ ~

CHAPTER 48
Five Emotional Intelligence Traps

Excess of everything, they say, is bad. I have learnt it the hard way by going overboard on reading content on emotional intelligence(EI). Daniel Goleman, Marcus Buckingham, Richard, Anne- you name it, I can boast of having read it. But it has had its own consequences, which I would call the emotional intelligence traps. Let us see what are these.

1-Hammer-Nail Trap

"If all you have is hammer, everything looks like a nail." Armed with so much reading, you feel like the maestro of emotional intelligence. Like yellow to a jaundiced eye, everything-big or small, appears to be an emotional intelligence issue. So you failed, blame EI, he failed, blame EI, project failed blame EI. You become so adept in finding non-existent emotional issues that you can find hidden agendas in a totally calm situation. You start ascribing motives to others and sulk or make others sulk, depending on whether you are an introvert or extrovert. You make emotional intelligence your core competence, without any such need. You tend to become the global honorary counselor or Judge, as the situation demands.

2-Guinea-Pig Trap

God save your colleagues-seniors, juniors or peers. Since you have adorned this mantle of emotionally intelligent wizard, every other person is a guinea-pig for you. Even they won't know their psyche as well as you claim to know. Give way Freuds and Jungs of the world, the new-age messiah of corporate psychology has arrived. He can analyse your behaviour in a jiffy and come up with life-changing suggestions, if you are interested by chance. What is happening to his life is immaterial, since he has condescended to make the world a better place to live in by his benevolent psycho-analysis of willing and unwilling volunteers. You are the mice in his larger scheme of things, or Guinea-pigs if you prefer.

3-Silo Trap

To an emotionally intelligent person, all the world can be divided into silos. There can be fifty shades of black and white for him, with no greys. Every person is a Type-A,...Type-Z or a weird combination of letters-INFJ, PQXY and so on. He will assign the silo to you and you the mortal will be stuck there for life in his eyes. It does boomerang at times, as I experienced myself. Impressed with Discover your strengths, I started matching the strength-types with my colleagues. I did find uncanny similarities. But I overdid it. I shared the observations about a colleague with him and encouraged him to read it for himself and gave my book to him. I got the shock of my life, when he sheepishly told me that the personality-type I assigned to him, in fact described one of our mutual hate-subjects (read boss). So in nutshell I branded him as the younger version of our senior. Boom!!!

4-Trending-theory trap

If you are old enough like me, you have been through different phases of emotional intelligence theories. Ego-states, Transactional analysis, Neuro-Linguistic Programming, Emotional Quotient, mindfulness and so on. Problem with these trending theories and fads, like other management concepts, is you end up believing the latest theory as the be-all and end-all on the subject, what with the empirical studies of so-many thousand managers. You become enamoured with the latest theory, till a new theory comes to the fore and postulates a new approach altogether. Who said life at work is easy.

5-The Narcissist Trap

The world revolves around you, I-me-myself becomes your success mantra. Since you have acquired the half-knowledge by eating & drinking the books, you deserve to be the centre of attraction of all and sundry. What if each has his own life to live, they can not cough, sneeze or yawn, without you being related to it, directly or indirectly. You have acquired the birthright to earn respect and recognition, attention and adulation, information and intimacy and the whole baggage of privileges you can think of. You are the master of the universe, king of the jungle and the supreme lord of corporate world. God is okay, but not a leaf should move without your will.

So, after having been trapped in all these traps for long, I have decided to take a sabbatical from emotional intelligence for the time being, and gorge books on other subjects that will be reflected by the slant of my writing in future posts.

Another new emotional intelligence book in the market, you say, gimme a break, for now at least. I will come to it, when I come to it.

~ ~ ~

CHAPTER 49
Five Management Lessons from a rabbit

Early this year, we brought a rabbit to our home and observing him as a pet for last few days made me think of lessons we can learn from him as a manager. Here are these lessons

1. Fake it till you make it

I don't know if you have seen a rabbit sitting in a relaxed position on its side from close quarters, but it surely gives the appearance of a lion sitting outside its den. Now call me stupid for making such a comparison but can't help the observation while looking at the rabbit. So it does behave like a fearless king of the jungle when it is in a relaxed state of mind. Now there can be no better description of the behaviour than to say-fake it till you make it. There is an extension to this, i.e. fake it till you become it, but that won't apply here. So we will make do with fake it till you make it. In work environment, even if you scared like hell, try pretending the fake. I know from personal experience it does give you confidence.

2. Always be on alert

I googled for rabbit speak to fully enjoy the pet experience and I found that rabbit's ears are like antennas. We can learn from their position-backward, forward, erect etc. what state of mind rabbit is in. Now you can't develop flexible ears like a rabbit but the point to learn here is to be always attentive and alert to your surroundings. As they say we must always keep our eyes and ears open. At workplace, even if you don't want to be a part of office politics, there is no harm to being alert to what is happening around you. Information is power and if you are alert, you can avoid many untoward incidents and nip many problems in the bud.

3. Celebrate Accomplishments

One other typical rabbit behaviour is that when it is well-fed, well-treated, well-placed, in other words, when it gets what it wants, it takes no time in expressing its pleasure. It starts jumping, leaping and running excitedly to show that it is happy. Initially we thought we gave him something wrong to eat, but when we researched we found that it is a sign of its happiness. So at workplace, whenever you or your team members accomplish something-big or small, do make it a point to celebrate the achievement and accomplishment.

4. Have trust in those who care for you

It is really amazing how a small animal who can run so fast that you can never catch him, sits steadily most of the time if you want to pick him up and pat him, play with him. No doubt, this might happen with other pets also, but I can share my own experience as a first-time pet owner. So once you approach him and pick him up, it will let you do that. This complete trust it places in you is almost like blind faith. It makes you protective of him. Wish we could have such trust at our workplaces. But maybe humans are more treacherous with humans, than animals. Just maybe.

5. Be clear in what you want

At least in its food habits, rabbit is really very demanding and single-minded. If it likes wheat-grass, it likes it. If it wants salty snacks, it wants them. You give him 100 times costly and better and healthy things, it won't budge. Just a sniff and your best laid plans are thrown away. If it likes it, well and good, if it does not, you can not make him like it. Wish we could all be so clear and focussed in what we wanted in our lives and our work-places. We could have achieved much more.

~ ~ ~

CHAPTER 50

Three Things in formative years that shape work-life

I was reading this column by Paulo Coelho today on the animal kingdom and lessons that we can learn from it, and it rang bells in the management thinking corner of my mind. Let us see what the three animals teach us

1-Initial induction makes us or breaks us

I have always shared this with my team members that if you can work sincerely and smartly for initial 4-5 years of your work life, rest becomes easier. You get branded as a committed, intelligent manager and then the ride is smooth. There are even times when you are not able to give your 100 per cent in later years for some reasons, but no one will doubt your intentions. Your small mistakes will be ignored based on your past track record. Such is the significance of initial years. But if we are unfortunate in these years and we get seniors who keep us in restraints and don't let us grow, we get stamped as status quoists and losers and this tendency sticks to us even in later years.

Coelho gives the example of elephant.

2-Hard taskmasters are good in the long run

Most of us would have worked with headstrong bosses, hard taskmasters, tough nuts and what nots. We would have definitely hated them for being so fussy, nit-pickers, micromanagers and heartless devils. But again once we are past those initial years and we introspect on our professional development and personal growth in retrospect, we would find ourselves being lucky to have those same bosses in the initial years. Because they drilled the good habits in us even at the cost of their image and perception.

Coelho gives the example of mother giraffe

Reminds of some ex-boss?

3-Bigger the pond, bigger the lessons

Some people do prefer to have bigger posts in small organizations, but let me tell you, working in a big organization and big vertical has its own rewards. For one, the exposure is big, challenges are bigger and you have scope to grow personally and professionally. I know from personal experience. When I was in corp comm of one unit, I did get to learn many things but it was all small scale. And when I moved to the corporate office, everything was bigger. I started handling ad releases of one crore in a day. Marketing people will release 25-30 lakh worth ad space on my word. It was a big kick. I knew that it was more credit to the organization I worked for, but still the adrenalin rush in managing big ad releases, managing last minute crisis situations was fun to say the least. I never realized I had this enterprising side in me until I experienced it.

Coelho explains this with the example of Koi fish.

Carps anybody!!!

~ ~ ~

About the Author

Sanjay was born in 1971 in Sonipat, Haryana (India). He has around 25 years of work experience in insurance and steel sectors in the domain of corporate communication and administration. The book is based on experiences he himself had and also the experiences shared by friends and acquaintances. A self-proclaimed introvert and avid reader, he tried to seek answers to his dilemmas at work and in other parts of life, from various sources. His quest for peace of mind for himself resulted in these writings which reflect on various aspects of Work-Life Balance.

Share you feedback and queries at gorask@gmail.com

~ ~ ~

.

www.ingramcontent.com/pod-product-compliance
Lightning Source LLC
Chambersburg PA
CBHW020503030426
42337CB00011B/214